Peggy and Molly

be kind, be humble, be happy

JULIETTE WELLS

EBURY
PRESS

Contents

Introduction

On a sunny spring day in September 2020 my partner and I were out walking Peggy, our lovable staffy, at the local dog park when we found a baby magpie alone on the ground. After waiting to see if its mother would return, we brought the bird home and nursed it back to health.

When this little fledgling first swooped into our lives, Peggy was unsure about the feathered visitor – but to our surprise she started to take on the role of nurturer, and before we knew it they were inseparable.

They would play ball, fall asleep while snuggling and lie in the sun together. Peggy was incredibly patient and gentle with her new best friend as the baby magpie continued to heal and grow. When it became clear that the tiny bird would be a permanent member of the family, we decided to call it Molly. You can imagine our reaction when Molly's baby feathers fell out and the new ones came in, and we discovered that he was a boy!

Molly loved to do whatever Peggy did, including barking, which we thought was adorable. When we shared their antics on social media, we discovered we weren't the only ones who had fallen in love with them.

In August 2021 Peggy had a litter of pups, and we decided to keep the only girl and call her Ruby. Molly and Ruby were destined to be close as Molly's singing had no doubt echoed through Peggy's stomach during her pregnancy, and he was eagerly waiting nearby at the birth to welcome the new additions into the world.

Peggy took a back seat for a while and watched Ruby and Molly play together for hours until their connection became just as strong.

The trio might be the most unlikely friends you have ever seen, but their bond will never be broken. We hope everyone can learn a little something from their deep affection for each other, and from the advice and life lessons they share in this book.

Peggy
and
Molly

Some souls understand each other the moment they meet.

They love with all their heart.

ENJOY
THE SAME
ACTIVITIES.

And know that the best tune to listen to is the song in their own heart.

A **FRIEND** MAY NOT REMEMBER **EVERYTHING** YOU SAY, BUT THEY'LL ALWAYS **REMEMBER** HOW YOU MADE THEM **FEEL**.

In any case, some things don't need to be said.

SOMETIMES IT'S ENOUGH TO HAVE A PAW TO CRY ON.

perspective. A true friend will help you see life from a different

They will remind
you there is
love, acceptance
and unity in
differences.

And that a gentle
smile and a kind
heart can go a
long way.

With a true friend, you can let your guard down.

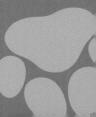

AND YOU CAN BE
THE **SUNSHINE**
IN **EACH** OTHER'S
WORLD.

YOU CAN SHOW
THEM **THEY**
MATTER BY PAYING
ATTENTION AND
LISTENING.

And you can be an example for generations to come.

Without losing your sense of fun.

PROTECT THE THINGS THAT MATTER MOST.

ALWAYS TRY
TO BE THE **REASON**
SOMEONE DOESN'T
FEEL **ALONE**.

Eat, snuggle, play, repeat.

And pause before you speak; you can't rewind your words.

WE **ALL**
HAVE A
DIFFERENT
POINT
OF **VIEW**.

A problem shared . . .

...IS A
PROBLEM
HALVED.

SO LET'S DO THIS **TOGETHER.**

Friends are there to help you with the things you can't do alone.

OR THE **THINGS** YOU DON'T WANT TO DO **ALONE**.

A friend will remember to share, even if it's their last worm.

BECAUSE THEY KNOW
KINDNESS DOESN'T **COST**
A THING YET IS **WORTH**
MORE THAN **ANYTHING**
YOU CAN BUY.

Sometimes just doing nothing soothes the soul.

REMEMBER **NOT**
EVERYONE IS
A **MORNING PERSON**.

Just because you're ready for the day, doesn't mean we all are.

TRY TO **FOCUS** ON THE **POSITIVES.**

Breathe in peace.

BREATHE
OUT
LOVE.

BE **STILL** AND **LISTEN** AND THE **ANSWERS** WILL **COME**.

JUST BE
YOU.

We all have bad days.

SO, **KEEP** YOUR CHIN **UP**.

And when
life gets hard,
cuddle.

BE READY TO
FACE LIFE'S
CHALLENGES
HEAD ON.

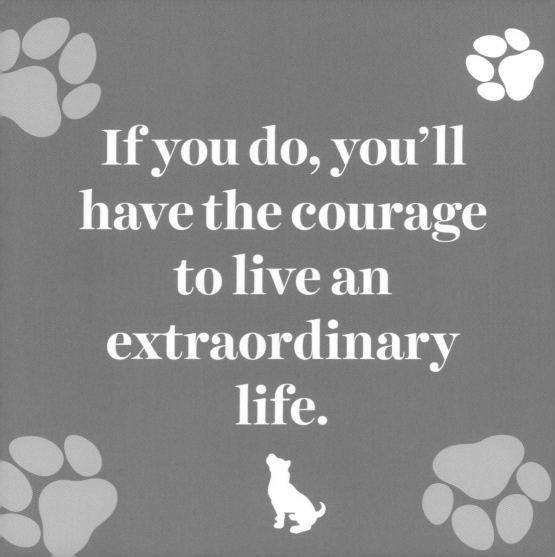

If you do, you'll have the courage to live an extraordinary life.

SHOW THE WORLD
YOU CAN BEFORE
IT **TRIES** TO
CONVINCE YOU
THAT **YOU** CAN'T.

SURROUND
YOURSELF WITH
FRIENDS WHO
MAKE YOU
SMILE FROM THE
INSIDE.

Because we become just like the people we hang out with.

SO BE BRAVE, STAND TALL.

TRY TO STAY
CURIOUS.

LET YOUR
JOY FLOW
ABUNDANTLY.

Dare to dream.

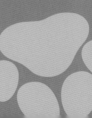

SPREAD
YOUR WINGS
AND WATCH
EVERYTHING
CHANGE.

Keep your nose out of everyone else's business.

GIVE YOUR
FRIENDS SPACE
WHEN THEY
NEED IT. . .

...but
remember:
together you
are stronger.

TRY TO RISE
ABOVE
LIFE'S
WORRIES.

AND **FOCUS** ON
THIS ONE **SPECIAL**
MOMENT. LET
EVERYTHING
ELSE GO.

YOU CAN BE
SMALL BUT
STILL HAVE
A **BIG HEART**.

Watch out for one another.

IT'S OKAY TO **ASK** FOR **HELP** WHEN YOU **NEED** IT.

Be grateful for those in your life.

LOVE
UNCONDITIONALLY.

Be kind,
be humble,
be happy.

Acknowledgements

This adorable book has been a collaborative venture, and I am deeply grateful to the individuals and organisations who have contributed their time, patience and expertise to help make it possible.

To the man who introduced me to the world of staffies, Reece, for your support and encouragement – thank you for your understanding during countless days devoted to capturing beautiful photos and the creative energy that comes with it all. It has been incredible watching your dedication and love for Molly, Peggy and Ruby, and how you embraced the public eye even though it wasn't in your nature.

To my circle of friends and family, Desiree Fraser, Naomi Cah and Michelle McKinney, who have been my moral support and encouragement – I appreciate your feedback, contribution and inspiration along the way.

To Frances Munro, who had a meaningful impact on my life's journey, for believing in me and for being a huge contributor to my growth as a person – I am forever grateful to you.